MASS FOR NANKING'S 1937

Also by New Academia Publishing

INSIDEOUTSIDE: Poems, by Sue Silver

NO BARKING IN THE HALLWAYS: Poems from the Classroom, by Ann Bracken

AT THE END OF THE SELF-HELP ROPE: Poems , by Ed Zahniser

THE HOUR OF THE POEM POEM: Poems on Writing, by David Bristol

THE WHITE SPIDER IN MY HAND: Poems, by Sonja James

THE ALTAR OF INNOCENCE: Poems, by Ann Bracken

THE MAN WHO GOT AWAY: Poems, by Grace Cavalieri

IN BLACK BEAR COUNTRY, by Maureen Waters

ALWAYS THE TRAINS: Poems, by Judy Neri

Read an excerpt at **www.newacademia.com**

MASS FOR NANKING'S 1937

Synchronizing Musics and Tonal Rhyming onto Poetry

Wing-chi Chan

NEW ACADEMIA PUBLISHING
SCARITH
Washington, DC

New Academia Publishing 2016

Printed in the United States of America

Library of Congress Control Number: 2015947705
ISBN 978-0-9864353-9-3 paperback (alk. paper)

SCARITH An imprint of New Academia Publishing

NEW ACADEMIA PUBLISHING

New Academia Publishing
PO Box 27420, Washington, DC 20038-7420
info@newacademia.com - www.newacademia.com

Contents

Foreword

Grateful to Wing-chi Chan's Confrontation For The 1937 Rape of Nanking

The 1937 rape of Nanking by the Japanese Imperial army is one of those historical events which defy linguistic modifiers; "tragedy" or "atrocity" do not approach the sadistic nihilism, the scale and scope, the wanton intensity of the horror. The cold anonymity of the atomic bombing of Hiroshima and Nagasaki might be the flip side of such inhumation, but there is something so massively perverse, so hands-on about the Nanking horror that makes us wonder what kind of species we are part of.

Wing-chi Chan's poetic eulogy, Mass for Nanking's 1937, is a courageous attempt to bring our senses to the charnel sensuality of the event. He applies his musician's ear to the words his eye calls forth. Any such protracted monstrous event could only be imagined with a certain surreal dissonance, and that is what Wing-chi has drafted for us. The poem moves from a calm and rational conception to an appropriately grotesque wildness. By the end of the first section to the poem's end, his words join together in a logic only those dark places in our subconscious that we seldom peek into can parse. It asks, how does one face what one cannot bear to see? But face these things we must if we are to excise them from human behavior. I am grateful to Wing-chi Chan for the confrontation.

—*A. B. Spellman, Poet & Witness to Jazz.*
Former Deputy Chairman, U.S. National Endowment for the Arts

Wing-chi Chan's Poetry Making a Statement of Global Partnership

I understand Wing-chi Chan's poetry as making a statement about "global partnership" as an alternative to any monocultural "globalization," as he himself suggests in a note to one of these poems. Rather than trying to be typically American poems, these experimental soundscapes investigate what emerges when English words are deployed in complex musical shapes derived from both Western European and Chinese models. The result will astonish even many intrepid readers.

Contextualizing these as experimental soundscapes may help domesticate that astonishment, however. After all, the sound poems of Hugo Ball and Wassily Kandinsky are a century behind us now, and the sound-intensive precisions and investigations of Louis Zukofsky are nearly as long-established. These pieces of Chan's typically reveal meanings – messages they can even insist on – so they are not pure sound, like Ball's; but they manipulate English with abandon, as Zukofsky did in his phonic translations of Catullus. In some ways, Chan's range of diction may surpass even Zukofsky's, as it includes archaic words ("ye" makes several appearances), rough dialects ("de" stands in for "the" whenever it sounds better), and neologisms. That the poems employ full, internal, and near rhymes, often use mirror-rhyme stanza structures, and shuffle words and phrases through multiple permutations, gives them an almost unworldly air. These are poems that will never be exhausted in simply a single reading.

It's as music, above all, that these poems wish to engage us. Naming the musical terms simply in the titles of these poems produces a long list: motif, song, ballet, symphony, tone, appassionata, aria, concerto, theme & variations, counterpoint, fugue, mass, minuet, arpeggio, fantasia, cantabile, cadenza, sonatina, and recitative. A professional musician, conductor, and organizer—might as well call him an impresario!—Chan has the background to make a serious effort to link Chinese and Western modes. Few among his readers will bring the same knowledge base to this project.

—*David McAleavey, Ph.D.*
Professor of English, George Washington University

Wing-chi Chan Is Liberated

There could be intellectual arguments about the governability of language and whether or not its only purpose is to articulate a clear message. This is not Wing-chi Chan's intent. Chan writes poems worthy of a field of discussion. Sometimes they are drawn biographically; other times they pose interesting historical questions; but, always the writing is bold, varied and heroic in new forms. Chan dares to literalize a contest of forces—not only Eastern and Western thought, but by poetry coupled with music. He liberates language with complex animation creating sonic landscapes.

Chan's art is to disrupt and connect, to disturb and delight. His emotional vocabulary comes from eastern thought flavored with western classical music. This is unique but will find its way to the reader. Ideas that are new will always be outside the norm of what is expected. Chan dramatizes ideas with spontaneous pleasure. His artistic identity is like no other. It's a sensory world come alive through poetry. His choices are alternative ones. He is liberated.

—*Grace Cavalieri, Poet.*
Producer/Host "The Poet and the Poem from the Library of Congress"

Preface

Synchronizing Musics and Tonal Rhyming onto Poetry

For the past eight years, I have been focusing on conceptual art, minimalism and pointillism music with synchronization profile and tonal rhyming perception in composing English poetry. Hence I crystallized a personal style that integrates English rhetoric with Italian musical terms and non-traditional rhyming words, which are cumulatively toned within and sublimed from an aesthetics of selfhood for de-normativity—Designing a passionate but allusive poetic architecture that aims at visualizing a cadenza, that touches the keyboard of my unsung concerto, that is textured upon a broad cross-cultural spectrum that orchestrates the inner voices of a diverse life journey.

During the late 1960s, I attended high school in Hong Kong, a colony of the United Kingdom at the time. There, I self-taught Grade VIII Certificate for Music Theory through the London-based Associated Board of the Royal Schools of Music system, a course parallel to a bachelor degree program's music curriculum. Under that system, learners were required to master the art of matching rhythmic accents, articulation, vowels and consonants of English texts with the melodic contour in music composition. Subsequently being a school teacher, vocalist, musicologist/ethnomusicologist, and choral conductor for a passage of forty years, I have practiced diction from singing English oratorio, German lieder, Italian operatic arias, and traditional Chinese operatic and narrative songs. Meanwhile, I focus my vision on the totality of sonic chemistry.

Along my career as an arts administrator and linguist in the Washington metropolitan area, composing classical Chinese poetry has become a part of my life since June of 1989. For thousands of years, classical Chinese poetry was guided by a specific range of tonal rhyming. Integrating with multiple cultures and disciplines, I struggled to form a serial structure in composing my own English poems, which combines disparate concepts of the twelve tone technique for atonal music, i.e. a linear order of transformation and the prime, inversion, retrograde, and retrograde-inversion. Consequently, I am inspired by I-Ching, a pillar of Chinese philosophy, in which the "Yin-Yang" integration is the foundation for the core structural organization on self-sensuality, spacing, contrast and balance.

—Chan, Wing-chi

First Paragraph on Each of the Six Stanzas of *A FUGUE OF TONE RHYMING*

(I) [Prime Passage]
Sound of passion muting thy voices for up-tune,
bound beyond ocean fluting joyance from moon.
Blessing ever via theme of nightie rain,
questing to lightly dream never in vain.
Link me to no other ties,
in blinking, Noah's eyes.

(II) [Retrograde with Modification]
Tune up thy voices muting by passion thru sound.
From moon, joyance fluting beyond ocean bound.
Rain via nightie themes of ever blessing,
never in vain, dreams lightly in questing.
Tie me to no other link,
to Noah's eye blinking.

(III) [Transform the Retrograde Passage for a > Shaped Effect]
Tie me to no other link.
Rain via nightie themes of ever blessing,
Tune up thy voices muting by passion thru sound.
From moon, joyance fluting beyond ocean bound.
Never in vain, dream lightly for questing,
to Noah's eye blinking.

(IV) [Transform the Retrograde Passage for a < Shaped Effect]
From moon, joyance fluting beyond ocean bound.
Never in vain, dream lightly for questing,
to Noah's eye blinking.
Tie me to no other link,
rain via nightie themes of ever blessing,
Tune up thy voices muting by passion thru sound.

(V) [Transform the Prime Passage for a > Shaped Effect]
Link me to no other ties.
Blessing ever via theme of nightie rain,
sound of passion muting thy voice being up-tuned.
Bound beyond ocean fluting joyance from a moon,
questing to lightly dream never in vain.
In blinking, Noah's eyes.

(VI) [Transform the Prime for a < Shaped Effect]
Bound beyond ocean fluting joyance from a moon,
questing to lightly dream never in vain.
In blinking, Noah's eyes.
Link me to no other ties.
Blessing ever via theme of nightie rain,
sound of passion muting thy voice being up-tuned.

First Paragraph on Each of the Six Stanzas of FUGUE OF TONE RHYMES

(1) [Dune Passage]
Sound of passion muting thy voices for up-tuned,
bound beyond ocean flitting loyance morn moon,
Blessing ever via theme of mighty tune,
questing to lightly dream never in vain,
Link me to no other lies
in blinding Noah's eyes.

(2) [Recognized with Neurognition]
[illegible] thy voice mute my passion [illegible]
[illegible] moon, loyance flitting [illegible]
[illegible]
[illegible]
[illegible]
[illegible]

[illegible]

[illegible]
[illegible]
[illegible]
[illegible]
[illegible]
[illegible]

[illegible]
[illegible]
[illegible]

[illegible]
Theme to no other [illegible]
[illegible]
[illegible]
[illegible]
[illegible]
[illegible]
[illegible]
[illegible]
questing to lightly dream never in vain,
[illegible]

(6) [Transformational [illegible] Shape, [illegible]]
Bound beyond ocean flitting loyance morn moon,
questing to lightly dream never in vain,
in blinding Noah's eyes.
Link me to no other lies.
Blessing ever via theme of mighty tune,
sound of passion muting thy voice being up-tuned.

Acknowledgements

In the months marking the 70th anniversary of the end of the Second World War…

To my grandparents, parents and senior relatives/teachers/friends who had experienced life-long human pain through one of the bloodiest periods of the twentieth century,

To my teachers, siblings, family, peers and students who, from time to time, have shared their bitterness and joy, pain and passion with me over a passage of life encountering with cross-oceanic and cross-strata conflict and compromise,

To Grace Cavalieri, David McAleavey and A.B. Spellman, Anna Lawton of New Academia Publishing, brothers and sisters, who have helped make this book available to the public,

To Mr. Li Zi-jian 李自健 , for his kind permission to use his remarkable art work *Nanjing Massacre* for the book cover and Joan Wong for her art work in preparing the cover design, and Huy Max Nguyen for his photography,

I am sentimentally indebted.

Wie Melodien zieht es mir leise durch den Sinn
Libera me, Domine, De morte aeterna

Passionate Messages in Chinese

<山河熱血濃>---調寄沁園春
曉月盧溝，刁斗沙風，漏夜急衝.
薊北刀光颯，兜頭劈殺，鬼神驚煞，土赤泥紅.
八一三魂，四行倉庫，旗正飄飄敵愾同.
金陵恨，懦夫遺弱女，倭獸逞凶.
江山半壁城空，浩氣燕歌夷狄動容.
嗣台兒莊捷，穿湘入蜀，流亡千里，扶老携童.
瀝膽長沙，仁安羌役，還我山河熱血濃.
盟軍識，芷江英雄劍，銘鑄青龍.

<攬月狂歌>
穿洋擊筑煞濤聲　　誰吻流星冷雨馨　　攬月狂歌哀國是　　去留肝膽一刀傾

—Chan, Wing-chi 陳詠智

MASS FOR NANKING'S 1937

Stanza I

The butcher--
hands on bone flipping,
boned through like combs,
every single park bloodied by gun,
knifed to cave after cave of wounding,
a Messiah's frame, mad overturned thunder,
12-13-1937 for Japan in years of our memorization,
irrelevant pen it mini-civilized, year off civilization,
of an Emperor's name, a flag turned blunder,
life under wave over wave of pounding,
below a darkened and wrinkle sun,
stone flown to bits by bombs,
a land in blood weeping--
The rupture.

Seven weeks,
thousands of hundreds,
even many minor, females,
a page of devil lines recalled--
Raped under chilled katana by a gang of killers.
The female-homed samurai,
male deformed in volunteer.
Being shaped shielded agenda bang for healers,
stage for de civil signs scored--
junior/senior, not only males,
thousands of millions,
seventy years.

*Katana was a sword used by Japan's army officers during the Second World War.

Weep,
with peers,
underground passion of rings,
pain never make past saddened alone,
moon's cold long badly atoned a country,
emotion of the rape harked by map wrapping,
year 2007 torched against sin under global integrity.
Hear heaven's vocal sincerity torching with dignity,
a nation to shape among marks of gap lapping,
wound's old song sadly toned each entry,
an ever main pick for a heartened tone,
extra-sound of lotion on strings,
with no fears--
A rip.

Dears, thou unrested--
Let hearing renew: Tone to heal, stone peeled, thy tear sealed.
Dears, be rested.

Stanza II

Japan in years of memorization for nineteen thirty-seven,
pounding wave over wave of bombs/stones on life.
In name of Emperor, under the flag,
sun turned to wrinkle and dark.
Bone, after butcher's hand,
flipping.
Weeping
blood upon ruptured land,
gun overturned each single park,
framed as Messiah, thunder of mad.
Wounding cave after cave, combed bones by knife,
pen it a year off civilization, mini-civilized be irrelevant.

Recalling lines of devil page:
Hundreds of the thousands,
females, even de minors,
weeks for seven,
gang raped--
under de killers' chilled katana.

Samurai homed from female,
volunteer deformed as a male.

New healers' shielded agenda:
Bang shaped--
Years for seventy,
females/males/seniors,
over millions of thousands,
scoring signs for a civil stage.

Global integrity torched against sin in two thousand seven.
By emotion, wrap up such map being harked of rape,
weep with peers for rings of passion underground.
A country atoned bad long by de cold moon,
saddened past never make de pain
alone...

Tone,
heartened pick thou an ever-main,
toned each entry of sad song off old wound.
Rip, with no fears, strings in lotion of extra-sound.
Of a nation, lapping over gap marked among shape,
Vocal sincerity with torch accompanied a dignity up heaven.

Unrested thou dears--
We do hear: May our tone, peel the stone, seal thy tear.
Be rested, dears.

[December 13, 2007; revised in 2010]

(Original Message in Chinese)

<金陵祭>
天涯咫尺祭金陵　　簫管壓弦傾輓情
起板招魂冤不息　　落紅離岸覓淒聲

Note: Heading toward the 70th Anniversary of Nanking Massacre Memorial Concert, we, the American team, arrived in Nanjing on December 11 at 1 AM after a bus trip of five hours from Shanghai Airport. I got the score on the same day at 12 noon. Our twelve American singer teammates listened to the local orchestra (comprised of additional players from Korea, Russia, Hong Kong, Singapore, Macao and Taipei) and choir's second rehearsal at 1 PM under MuHai Tang's baton the same day on Dec 11. I waited until 4 PM to coach the first rehearsal for our American singer team -- from reciting the romanized Chinese song text to running through the score and practicing by parts; I was completely relieved by 5:30 PM when we finished our first but only rehearsal. By that time, I knew we would be ready! Suddenly the accompanist student from Beijing pointed to our tenor teammate and said, "I got your DVD." At this moment, I then realized that Thomas Young, a faculty of Sarah Lawrence College, came to sing with the local choir for this memorial concert without telling his soloist status as one of America's three best known tenors. The first concert was doing fine on the 12th. By December 13, everybody voiced out fully moving on the stage. Together with Tang on the podium, I, as the choir conductor, thanked in tears under the audience's repeated standing ovation. Returning to hotel, I was not able to sleep while my ears were in echo of the first song that I learned from my father (who worked for *The Flying Tiger* in 1942)—*"Defend The Yellow River"*; I drafted a poem and continuously revised it that eventually expanded into a two-stanza *"Mass"*.

A COUNTERPOINT FOR YANGTZE AND HUDSON RIVERS

Dedicated to Professor Chou Wen-Chung

Stanza I

In sequence,
pressing on millions under fear
filmed for the Chinaman fantasia,
off-tuned premium of New West's integrity.
Thou young never mused with peers instrumental for Olympic.
Yangtze, river here, ever used to contrapuntal cum an epidemic.
Opium ruined across Old East's sovereignty,
down-named de Sick Man of Asia,
multi-powers' crashing sphere
of influence.

"And the Fallen Petals",
handing forms via sunflower,
orchestrated passion in miniature,
scoring over an Ocean, by one young clever.
Recalling forever, a nation's wounded River,
penetrated station, infrastructure,
landing storms of gunpowder,
amid rubbles of metal.

Reverse pace
beyond financial favor,
porting on land with fan,
tone for theme of de cream,
step relieved on Hudson River,
shouldering multi-cultural passion,
wonder on Mosaic virtue of equality.
Under historic Statute of the Liberty,
heading toward municipal fashion,
map for stationing with silver,
clone over film of a dream,
sporting in band of men,
different ethnic color,
diverse race.

With no replacement,
off mud of unsung history,
share variety of single tone,
harking for a voice of dignity,
uproot form to another century,
siding cell hot for the flowery bud,
weep blessing fallen petal of ye fine,
no cease of gonging by free-will clever.
Kiss lines of tree along a tri-state River,
keep messing broken metal in mind,
inside melting pot of de new blood,
root from my mother's country,
marking choice of nationality,
bear variables of poly zone,
in flood for a sunk misery,
once in displacement.

Stanza II

Yangtze, a river here, ever used to contrapuntal cum epidemic.
Opium ruined across old East's sovereignty,
down-named de Sick Man of Asia,
multi-power's crashing sphere
of influence.
In sequence,
pressing on millions under fear
filmed for the Chinaman fantasia,
off-tuned premium of New West's integrity.
Thou young never mused with peers instrumental for Olympic.

Recalling forever, a nation's wounded River,
penetrated stations infrastructure,
landing storms of gunpowder
amid rubbles of metal.
"And the Fallen Petals",
handing forms via sunflower,
orchestrated passion in miniature,
scoring over an Ocean, by one young clever.

Under historic Statute of the Liberty,
heading toward municipal fashion,
map for stationing with silver,
clone over film of a dream,
sporting in band of men,
different ethnic color,
diverse race.
Reverse pace
beyond financial favor,
porting on land with fan,
tone for theme of de cream,
steps relieved on Hudson River,
shouldering multi-cultural passion,
wonder on Mosaic virtue of equality.

Kiss lines of tree along a tri-state River,
keep messing broken metal in mind,
inside melting pot of new blood,
root from my mother's country,
marking choice of nationality,
bear variables of poly zone,
in flood for a sunk misery,
once in displacement.
With no replacement,
off mud of unsung history,
share variety of single tone,
harking for a voice of dignity,
uproot form to another century,
siding cells hot for a flowery bud,
weep blessing fallen petal for ye fine,
no cease of gonging by free-will clever.

[Winter, 2008. Revised in 2010]

(Original Message in Chinese)

<冠 [文中易安] 伉儷詩恭賀八五壽慶>
文質彬彬賦九魂　中流滾滾表丹心
易從宮徵旋相變　安聽山濤憶故人

Note: Professor Chou Wen-Chung 周文中, an internationally recognized composer of the Twentieth Century, is a professor emeritus of Columbia University and a member of American Academy of Arts and Letters; he composed a triolet for orchestra "*And the Fallen Petals*" in 1955, tone-portraying his teenaged life experienced Japan's atrocities over the Yangtze Delta during the disastrous Sino-Japanese War, 1937-45; Chou, as an immigrant from China who later became naturalized in the United States, has been residing in New York city since 1949 and faithfully promoting global cultural partnership, other than a single-handed-cultural globalization.

MESMERIZED AT SIR ROBERT BLACK COLLEGE

A campus, coated of tall pine/vitalized over wind and sand,

targets, amid globe of academia, to cultivate de learnt man.

A tutorial legacy, in portraying multi-dimensions discourse,

mesmerized by court-to-court horticulture along silent zen.

[March, 2015, University of Hong Kong]

(Chinese Version)

〈賦柏立基院〉

柏松環校歷風塵
立足儒林斅學勤
基石彌堅容對問
院庭禪籟賦斯耘

Note: : The Hong Kong Medical College was founded in 1887, and later merged with the Colleges of Arts and Engineering to form the University of Hong Kong in 1911 by the British Colonial Government. Dr. Sun Yat-sen, father of the Republic of China in 1911, was a graduate of that Medical College. Ranked 42nd in the world by US News & Report, its main language of instruction remains to be English, even after Hong Kong's return to Socialist China in 1997.

LITTLE FACE

(A piece I composed to my daughter in 2005)

Twenty-two years ago, I worked as waiter in Chinese restaurant
while I was still at the graduate program in Baltimore.
One day I couldn't find a baby-sitter for you
and took you with me to work.
You were sitting with another girl
of same age and chatting
inside a restaurant kitchen.
Restaurant people praised you two were doing so fine,
and maturely calm with no trouble.
After the business time, I talked with the dishwasher
who was the girl's grandpa and learned that
the little pretty girl was the younger one
of a twin in the family.

At time when Viet Cong soldiers took control of southern Vietnam

Every port was packed with refugees like water flooding over dam

A family of three generations made all their belongings being gone

Trying to board on a boat for escaping out of de capital city Saigon

Cold-blood sea storm wrapped away from the group an elder sister

No hesitation rushing out to save little girl, first mother, then father

One by one, but none of these three persons could return thereafter

Upon arriving the States, grandfather advised little surviving sister

Believe you will meet your parents/sister in your coming days later

We've missed them for 22 years—been grateful being off from bitter

Dadad

[2005/Revised 2015]

A CLUSTER OF "5W + 1H" AND "ING" MOTIF

where's thy hometown
what else out of bound
when to make a pound
how pay to be unfound
why needs gum sound
who cares dumb count

off a I-phone news
ringing
with morning dews
winging
as a spacecraft pin
clinging
by cloud and wind
singing

[2014]

Note: Living under a system of being market-oriented, artists and literati, with dignity, are mostly speechless; I share the same kind of bitterness with them in breathing fresh air under the pressure of today's life.

DISTANT BLESSING FOR MOTHERS OF SILENT VICTIMS

For mothers whose gunless kids at a forbidden arena gunned to die
For thy heart already been tearing down and chilling tear being dry
For a passion over 9,125 days, your pain has been heard to be mine
For passage of twenty-five years, a ruling gang has ruled only at "I"
For rejecting to let de dignified spirits back to a civilian-ship on line
For butchers pee at propaganda that in-house laws not to be in trial
For the devil, endless fateful disasters shall rip upon his family side
For silent victims' mothers, may our distant blessing fly to your sky

[2014 Mother's day]

(Original Message in Chinese)

喪夫亡子眼枯煎　冷月無風魘夢纏
莫謂元兇逃法眼　障循家孽問青天

Note: On a Mother's Day, my daughters took their mom out for shopping. At McDonald by myself, I suddenly realized that many mothers have lost their kids over the past two decades under the devil's gun….

A PARTRIDGE'S WEEPING SONG

On wings of partridge's improvising for song,
in echo over mountains harmonizing of gong,
transforming a brother-pipe voice into mong.

On wings of a partridge's weeping song on blood,
let silvery-star river fall on man's green in flood,
not to give up even given on deep passion in mud.

Inspired from a poem by Zhang Hen Shui (1895-1967)
[2013]

(Original Chinese Version)

<浣沙溪> 张恨水
化為鷓鴣引興歌，這山歌(唱)那山和，化為鷓鴣叫哥哥。
化成鴣啼渾是血，人間碧落有銀河，人莫奈何奈情何。

Note: Zhang Hen Shui (also romanized as Chang Hen Shui), 1895-1967, a prolific Chinese novelist and poet, is relatively unknown among American scholars. He published more than 110 novels and large volumes of classical poetry in his 50 years of fiction writing. I am especially impressed by his use of realistic dialogue, parables and dream sequences to satirize the corrupt bureaucracy under his novels. He had a natural passion in portraying images under his poetry.

BALLET SHADOW MESMERIZED BY SYMPHONY STAR BRIGHT

Poetized under a keyboard of moonlight,
let's tone along rhyming river with wine.

best not to miss any ballet shadow on sky.
Mesmerized by symphony of star bright,

Let's paddle toward the torrent, over your tempest
for a spring evil king.

for musketeer to sing.
Bet nightingale will wet-kiss upon my naked chest

[2013]

(Chinese Version)

<嬋娟弄影清>
韻遊江月一樽倾　何負嬋娟弄影清
逆水行舟秋煞過　披襟還賦燕歌聲

A SOLILOQUY FOR JOHN BROWN AT HARPERS FERRY

A melodyless evening
A breathless lightning
A gong of rain stoning
A cello-note drowning
A un-phrased running
A no-keycenter tuning
A silent mark listening
A no-makeup morning

Life is hard at mid night
Heartened meet a bright
Voice flies, not with kite
Heart locked on this site
Hear victims' eye might
No fear fight as a knight
Blacken lights on height
Sunrise will let you light
Breathe above thou sight
Beyond a wrong or right

Over de 3-state water, master/ghost/fairy been dancing day to night

Over talk of multiple act, a no-word hug clicked on mindful message

Over team of 22 pioneers, thy first shot warred for 3 million of slave

Over shooting of secession, history names John Brown man of brave

Over de stormless, cute duck painted thou mind with peaceful image

Over voice of 150 years, an aria at Harpers Ferry for blood of a bright

Note: Harpers Ferry, a national park today, was a site where John Brown and his twenty-one followers tried to seize an arsenal for starting a freed-slave revolt in 1859. Their failed raid ignited the out-birth of the 1861-1865 Civil War.

ALONE, IN TONE

Who is the master along a freezing river?
High-note?
Fortissimo!
Pages of book?
Pianissimo!
Heartened attention,
dance on flawless variation,
off temptation,
freezing water sounds free from suffer!

Headtone lands on ice in lieu of sky,
beside one in de fable--
Who is peeper?
Who is deeper?
Mark of red and purple--
Drink alone for the flowing still fine,

I fish along a tiny freezing river,
millions of
purple-heart variation,
thousands
red-mark temptation,
nothing can
hook off my attention,
I smile for free from any suffer!

Alone, stage upon soundless/freezing water,
drink ice in lieu of bottles of rose wine,
hands on pianissimo
pages of--
aged book.
High note--
Lands from
head-tone fortissimo.
Steps dance along that flowing be fine--
In tone, beside who I am, who is the master? [5-11-2012]
(Images are based on an original Chinese version in 1968)
〈千紅奈我何〉
萬紫千紅奈我何　寒江垂釣笑呵呵　飲冰如酒風霜露　橫立激流慷放歌　[筆架山]

CAPITOL HILL & WALL STREET—THE GREED

We need job,
Capital killed--Wall Street.
SEC, thine saw off from $ monsters,
impotent Uncle Sam passed bill of stimulus,
silence independent investigation rushed to Capitol's affair.
Hard earning savings stolen--accumulator, refinance, conspirator--Hear!
E-Trade, big cheat to ye, me, he, she, people sea--cheat us not they been treated.
Under an eat-tray--We were betrayed by Capitol Hill and Wall Street, the greed.
Heart waning, bluffing, rotten--gladiator, defiance, prosecutor! Where?
Default, deficient de-regulatory flushing billions on warfare.
Omnipotent big $ still be the devil's bonus.
SOS! Suffering de on-law dumpsters.
Capitol sealed, just bullshit!
They're mob.

E-Trade, big cheat to ye, me, he, she, people sea--cheat us not they are treated.
Heart waning, bluffing, rotten--gladiator, defiance, prosecutor! Where?
Default, deficient de-regulatory flushing billions on warfare.
Omnipotent big $ still be the devil's bonus.
SEC, thine saw off from $ monsters.
Organized gang of Wall Street!
White House goes retreat--
Capital killed,
need job!
The mob--
Capitol sealed,
multi white mouse besieged,
Why our means/end never meet?
SOS! Suffering de on-law dumpsters,
impotent Uncle Sam passed bill of stimulus.
Silence independent investigation rushed to Capitol's affair.
Hard earning savings stolen--accumulator, refinance, conspirator-- Hear!
Under an eat-tray---We were betrayed by Capitol Hill and Wall Street, the greed.

[10-2011, New York City]

Note: As one of the so-called 99% victims of the 2008 financial scam, I was deeply moved by the civilian protesters' Occupy-Wall-Street peaceful movement in 2011…

APPASSIONATA ARIA ON PRAISING ....

moonlight thumbs onto thee pillow,
star-night hums with no choral,
drums ring off arc de sorrow,
concertizing your resilience,
along a vitalized silence,
for thou rejuvenation,
being blameless,
resonant joy,

river belted by curve of green grass,
strings melted on winds and brass,
sonic shaped beyond tone row,
makes peace off from fear,
a click pierced to wire,
for thy emancipation,
to be frameless,
dissonant boy.

steps on weeping rain and storm,
under mindful dedication,
by thine bitter smile,
mind beyond harm,
may brace....

behind the ripping pain but calm,
upon touchful motivation,
along thy rubble of tile,
touch with no arm,
let's praise....

boy braces,
frameless on eye,
rejuvenation mindful,
wires to pierce on a click,
silence concertizes a bitter smile,
calm de weeping rain under pillow,
brass choral thumbs ring off star-night,

joy praises,
blameless in mind,
emancipation touchful
off-fear from peace make,
resilience vitalizes rubble of tile,
storm ripping pain above arc de sorrow,
grass in green curve hums onto moonlight.

[March, 2011]

Note: Appassionata means passionate in Italian. It is also the name of one of Beethoven's three great piano sonatas of his middle creation period during 1803-6, remarkable for its immense power of lyrical melodic pulses in struggling for a simple but ideal image. Beethoven's hearing rapidly deteriorated during the time when he composed this piece.

A DUO CONCERTO FOR MOON & NOON

Dedicated to my 100-year-old- Grand-Teacher Professor Jao Tsung-I **饒宗頤**

Mountain over hill, shock and bust, passed behind my flight,
amidst cloud, torchable is silent, rhythmic noon,
hard melodizing a trusty rainbow across sky,
immeasurable miles above ground--
Prosodic theme.
Melodic dream--
Inseparable smiles beyond sound,
off heart, liberalized de dusty crossbow to fly,
torched to kiss the past resilient, pianismic moon,
cast montage of listen after view, rock and dust, on starlight.

Shy moon--
torches tonight's cloud, unkissable,
flies to lead crossbow off the rainy, dusty heart,
dreams beyond pianismic sound of inseparable smiles,
star listens to montage cast for lightsome dust, rock, by view.
My sight's passed over mountain behind bust/shock on a hill,
themes grounded on immeasurable of rhythmic miles,
sky synchronizes heartened, trusty rainbow hard,
proud amidst today's untouchable--
Shiny noon.

Melodic theme--
Inseparable smiles beyond sound,
off heart, liberalized de dusty crossbow to fly,
torched to kiss the past resilient, pianismic moon,
cast montage of listen after view, rock and dust, on starlight.
Mountain over hill, shock and bust, passed behind our flight,
amidst cloud, torchable is silent, rhythmic noon,
hard melodizing a trusty rainbow across sky,
immeasurable miles above ground--
Prosodic dream.

Star listens to montage cast for lightsome dust, rock, by view,
dreams beyond pianistic sound of inseparable smiles,
flies to lead crossbow off the rainy, dusty heart,
torches tonight's cloud, unkissable--
Pianismic moon.
Rhythmic noon--
Proud amidst today's untouchable,
sky synchronizes heartened, trusty rainbow hard,
themes grounded on immeasurable of rhythmic miles,
my sight's passed over mountain behind bust/shock on a hill.

[January 2010]

(Original Message in Chinese)

饒門絶學貫東西　宗仰敦煌擇竹棲　頤養儒丰宏往聖　師公德慧與丘齊

Note: Jao Tsung-I 饒宗頤, the first Asian sinologist awarded the title of Associate Foreign Member of the Académie des Inscriptions et Belles-Lettres, is a pioneering scholar of many fields in humanities, authoring a wide spectrum of topics in Chinese art, archeology, history, literature, and philology. His voluminous publications include over 80 books and 500 treatises. He is also a prominent Chinese poet, painter, qin-zither performer and calligrapher of the highest caliber.

THEME & VARIATIONS ON CURVE OF LIFE

Fool, quite coz',
dances on the click,
booming nerve as knife.
Mole pen pop, Hi-Fi moussed, turns immeasurable creature.
Cold den job, Wi-Fi housed, never be de measurable torture.
Zooming curve of a life,
trances on the lake,
cool , being los'.

Cold den job, Wi-Fi housed, never be de measurable torture,
zooming curve of a life,
trances on the lake,
being los'-- cool.
Quite coz'-- fool
dances on this click,
booming nerve as knife.
Mole pen pop, Hi-Fi moussed, turns immeasurable creature.

What to pay
percussively binding to weather,
fair enough to dwell via outer-surf pressing.
Farewell, no words, with inner-turf blessing,
abusively winding along feather,
not to stay.

Farewell, no words, with inner-turf blessing,
abusively winding along feather,
what to pay.
Not to stay,
percussively binding to weather,
fair enough to dwell via outer-surf pressing.

Mar
to correct a heartfelt
untold message mated for bunny.
With fist, minding the fine by high seal.
Under mist, binding eyes behind wheel,
folding a passage of late journey,
recollect hard-to-tell
scar.

Under mist, binding eyes behind wheel,
folding a passage of late journey,
recollect hard-to-tell
scar.
Mar
to correct a heartfelt
untold message mated for bunny.
With fist, minding the fine by high seal.

[2009]

Note: This was my first piece of poem exploring to create a yin-yang structure for the purpose of visualizing a mirroring effect. Subsequently I composed another poem, in the same year, with a thorough visual and sonic yin-yang architecture that has systematically regulated the contrast and balances of rhymes, length of words and lines, dynamics and shape, i.e. A FUGUE OF TONE RHYMING.

A FUGUE OF TONE RHYMING

(I)
Sound of passion muting thy voices for up-tune,
bound beyond ocean fluting joyance from moon.
Blessing ever via theme of nightie rain,
questing to lightly dream never in vain.
Link me to no other ties,
in blinking, Noah's eyes.

Leap to its lynch for the sun.
Lips, on de finch, sip thy bun.
Moon full, cooling narcotic sad,
gonging in echo side by side.
Tune up, cupping nostalgic tag,
longing for new tide after tide.

Recall foot-prints step over step,
falling onto set of mood in map.
Back to miles of an original,
track piled up of the natural.
Tone those behind claps with no fame,
alone on steps hide nothing to shame.

Forget long be on-line for real,
bet a song for the fine to seal.
Never in mind!
So never be mine?
In a sense, I find
only a clever dine.

Stuck up a single lay,
neither way to hate,
even no luck in fate.
By the bay,
wind up my day,
fold up what late to pay,
an untold fate to stay.

Behind a lingering tone,
refine my tingeing lone.
Heart of mine does hear:
The fine is always near.
Anything not clear? Cheers!

(II)
Tune up thy voices muting by passion thru sound.
From moon, joyance fluting beyond ocean bound.
Rain via nightie themes of ever blessing,
never in vain, dreams lightly in questing.
Tie me to no other link,
to Noah's eye blinking.

Sun, up to its lynch, for leap,
bun of a finch sipped by lips.
Narcotic sad cooling full moon,
tide after tide to renew for longing.
Nostalgic tag cupping up-tune,
side by side, in echo to de gonging.

Steps print in foot to recall.
A map in mood sets to fall.
An original miled from thy back,
the natural up piled for de track.
Fame those no claps behind tone,
shame nothing to hide step alone.

For real, on-line forgets so long,
to seal the fine for betting song.
Mind neither.
Finding me, in a sense, not either.
So mine be never?
Dine only with a clever.

Lay singles for stuck,
even nil with any luck.
Hate neither way,
With mate, not say--
The bay binding,
my day winding.
Pay late what up fold,
stay by fate, an untold.

Tone lingering behind,
lone tingeing a refined.
Hear: So by heart mine?
Near, always, is the fine.
Clear? Cheers!

(III)
Tie me to no other link.
Rain via nightie themes of ever blessing,
Tune up thy voices muting by passion thru sound.
From moon, joyance fluting beyond ocean bound.
Never in vain, dream lightly for questing,
to Noah's eye blinking.

Bun of finch, sipped by lips.
Nostalgic tag cupping up-tune,
side by side, in echo to de gonging.
Tide after tide to renew for longing,
narcotic sad cooling full moon.
Sun up to its lynch, for leap.

A map, in mood, sets to fall,
the natural up piled of thy track.
Shame nothing to hide stepping alone,
fame those no clapping behind a tone,
An original miled from de back,
steps print, in foot, to recall.

Mine be never,
so let thy mind not either!
For real, on-line forgets so long.
To seal the fine for betting song.
Finding my sense, neither.
Dine with clever?

The bay binding,
pay late what up fold,
hate neither way, lay singles for stuck.
With mate, not say--Nil with any luck.
Stay by fate, an untold.
My day winding.

Clear?
Lingering behind,
hear tone: So, by heart, mine?
Near the lone, always, is fine.
Tingeing a refined,
cheers!

(IV)
From moon, joyance fluting beyond ocean bound.
Never in vain, dream lightly for questing,
to Noah's eye blinking.
Tie me to no other link,
rain via nightie themes of ever blessing,
Tune up thy voices muting by passion thru sound.

Tide after tide to renew for longing,
narcotic sad cooling full moon.
Sun up to its lynch, for leap.
Bun of finch, sipped by lips.
Nostalgic tag cupping up-tune,
side by side, in echo to de gonging.

Fame those no clapping behind a tone.
An original miled from de back,
steps print, in foot, to recall.
A map, in mood, sets to fall,
the natural up piled of thy track.
Shame nothing to hide stepping alone.

To seal the fine for betting song,
Finding my sense, neither.
Dine with clever?
Mine be never,
so let thy mind not either!
For real, on-line forgets so long.

With mate, not say--Nil with any luck.
Stay by fate, an untold.
My day winding.
The bay binding,
pay late what up fold,
hate neither way, lay singles for stuck.

Near the lone, always, is fine.
Tingeing a refined,
Clear?
Cheers!
Lingering behind,
hear tone: So, by heart, mine!

(V)
Link me to no other ties.
Blessing ever via theme of nightie rain,
sound of passion muting thy voice being up-tuned.
Bound beyond ocean fluting joyance from a moon,
questing to lightly dream never in vain.
In blinking, Noah's eyes.

In gonging,
tune up thy cupping nostalgic tag,
in echo side by side, leap to a lynch for the sun.
New tide after tide, lips on de finch sip thy bun.
Moon full, a cooling narcotic sad,
by longing.

The map,
falling onto set of mood,
back to miles of an original,
tones those behind claps with no fame.
Alone on steps hide nothing to shame,
track piled up of the natural,
recall step on printed foot,
one step.

Never in mind,
not ever be mine!
Forget long be on-line for real.
Bet a song for the fine to seal.
Only a clever dine?
In sense, I find.

Neither way?
Even with no luck,
an untold fate stuck up a single bay.
Wind up my day on what late to pay.
Fold up the tuck,
let me stay.

Hear?
Heart of mine clear,
behind de lingering tone.
Refine my tingeing lone,
the fine does near.
Cheers!

(VI)
Bound beyond ocean fluting joyance from a moon,
questing to lightly dream never in vain.
In blinking, Noah's eyes.
Link me to no other ties.
Blessing ever via theme of nightie rain,
sound of passion muting thy voice being up-tuned.

New tide after tide, lips on de finch sip thy bun.
Moon full, a cooling narcotic sad,
by longing.
In gonging,
tune up thy cupping nostalgic tag,
in echo side by side, leap to a lynch for the sun.

Alone on steps hide nothing to shame,
track piled up of the natural,
recall step on printed foot,
one step.
The map,
falling onto set of mood,
back to miles of an original,
tones those behind claps with no fame.

Bet a song for the fine to seal.
Only a clever dine?
In sense, I find.
Never in mind,
not ever be mine!
Forget long be on-line for real.

Wind up my day on what late to pay.
Fold up the tuck,
let me stay.
Neither way?
Even with no luck,
an untold fate stuck up a single bay.

Refine my tingeing lone,
the fine does near.
Hear?
Cheers!
Heart of mine clear,
behind de lingering tone.

A MINUET OF DREAM

Music in score sounds to dream abroad,
plucking heart's new string
for vibrato touch.
A bel canto crutch
un-plugs an old heart's ring.
Tone in life rounds up a dreamy thought.

On wings of song under the moonlight,
hear n'thing by power,
thy ears at night.
Near the bright,
bear a th'nking tower,
long for a ring of blundering noon-bright.

String along vein on silky stream,
de single tower by heart,
envisions an insight,
on the road side.
Echo to low tide,
en-missions a bright,
beyond bingo power in part,
sing under rain for milky dream.

String on pizzicato for gold cream,
theme a light-tower's touch,
heart within old tune.
Ears under bold moon,
stream the dream onto such,
sing legato along streamlined beam,
a sold out dream.

[August 2007]

Note: The minuet is a specific dance music in Western Europe. Vibrato is a technique, where the left hand produces slight fluctuation of pitch on sustained notes by an oscillating motion that will give effects of microtonic embellishment and emotional quality of the tone. Bel canto is generally considered a highly artistic technique, focusing on the voice projection of head and chest tones. Pizzicato is a technique to pluck the strings by one or two fingers on the indicated notes. Legato is a different type of tone effect by playing without any perceptible interruption between the indicated notes.

ARPEGGIO ON MOON TO NOON

Lying on top of park by lagoon,
sip to hark for spoon of palm tea.
Teaism ripping dark off calm sea--
Thy flying dip pops up to a moon.

Minding for tomorrow's percussive light at noon,
blow on de long night's binding sight tone by tone.
Tiny nightingale's song flows onto bone over bone,
tows a mind off massive nightmare from typhoon.

Deploring moon with siren is due to night in dark,
long wound cut deep by sharp cone.
Song tunes up sleep in hub of tone,
exploring noon in silence for knight's limo to park.

Heading on map after map to find
a warm sun-bright piling at noon,
visualize storm of fun-bite soon,
leading to montage of spacing in mind.

Touching no dial phone with the old evil,
marking tone bowed with a boon,
lips never miss touch on de lark.
Moving on steps with toning mark,
space toned after a silent noon--
Touchy no longer tiled alone is bold civil.

[Summer, 2007]

Note: Arpeggio, means broken chord, is a musical technique for playing notes of a chord in rapid succession. When I went to graduate school in Lafayette, Louisiana in 1979, I often passed through quite a few lagoons on my way to class; or more specifically, they were lagune, or small, pond-like bodies of shallow water connected with a larger body of water. Teaism is the aesthetics of tea ceremony. Typhoon, phonetically akin to Chinese TaiFeng, is a violent tropical storm in the China sea and western Pacific area.

STURM UND DRANG: PULSING TONES IN LIFE

Old wound toned a messy passage for long,
young in scoring various tones
for life.
By knife,
furious core wounded to bones,
folded around toning message with no song.

Hence de knife being caged--
Stage by stage,
hill, round de mill.
Blowing and hipping,
coast to coast.
Where is thy hark?
Here's dog's bark.
For a toast,
keep flowing but skipping.
Lost an anchor bill,
heartened my chill—
Another life score paged.

Wash thy face being paled,
wrap up old map full of loot steps,
stepping on gap between boot taps,
facing to a rash of failed.

In score of notes in dark,
thy string of tones peel down a mound over de knife,
under rings of passion with bound in tear.
Upbringing ye lotion of sound with no fear,
stringing to tone on the seal for a new found in life,
one tiny core totes a lark.

[June 14, 2007]

Note: Sturm und Drang means storm and stress. It is an aesthetic style of the eighteenth century that referred to expressing one's sentiments through the use of unpredictable melodic contour, rapid changes of tempo and dynamics, and pulsing rhythms.

FANTASIA ON A STREAM OF DREAM

A stream folding of bubble lonely
sinking down a toned heart.
Blinking above stoned mart
a fold-up dream of double pony.

Over many streaming springs,
recall an old meadow,
refining for a long hark.
Shining songs by thy lark,
re-score a molded shadow,
call for stream below ye spring.

Pass de stream,
cast for a dream--
Nothing perish.
Ye diminishing fire cracked
from dip over dip of pine,
just burning.
No earning,
from sip after sip of wine,
the diminished burn clicked.
Just publish,
never vanish--
A stream of dream.

[May 2007]

Note: Fantasia is hereby being titled as an image in portraying a fanciful and dreamlike mood. By 2007, my stream of dream had been a passage of twenty eight years since I came to the United States in 1979…

A CANTABILE FOR ONE MORE MANTILLA ON WALL STREET

One more mantilla brushing over Wall Street,
fans off channel fox,
ever tasteful.
Never wasteful,
run to food on box
by a core wanderer rushing with none to meet.

Picking rice pieces,
full bow from a dustily-sealed lightest spot for thought
plucks thy heartstrings.
Being stuck to clings,
tow up de trustingly-healed highest hot of being sought,
ticking on priced peace.

The carry-out dinner,
down-beats the meal of mind in full course,
up-beats heal for minding of thou fool's loss,
for a hurry-foul runner.

Sipping a cup of pepo tea,
on side-walk,
the long passage,
in caulk
of song message,
at New York,
ripping off hub of people sea.

[April 2007]

Note: Mantilla is a silk scarf worn by Spanish ladies. Anchored by Wall Street, the New York City has been a colorful melting pot for adventurists, wanderers, immigrants, refugees and…

A CADENZA OF PASSION

Passed the time being,
    life, a perpetual passion,
  crossing to eventual station,
pass de ocean in timing.

Passionate for root from one ground,
landing on entry to entry--
  Land of another country,
thy foot passing beyond single bound.

Sounds fry up Dragon's cadenza of brilliance.
Hence eyed baton trances alone,
heart-strings dance with no clone.
Cry for cadence down off Draconian civiliance.

Homing perpetually beyond bound after bound,
rooted from timbre passion,
footing onto chordal motion,
each town eventually turns into a home ground.

  Life ascending by time--
Transcending with no dime.
    Cross the line for a new fine,
     pressing onto another station.
      Bless my fatherly passion--
  Across thy mind of de old wine.

[October 2006]

Note: Cadenza, in the traditional concerto, is a virtuoso passage played by a soloist to display his/her technical virtuosity in ornamentation or improvisation. This early piece allusively documented my first feelings of homesickness of "landing on entry to entry."

A SONATINA THEMED ON STARLIGHT

Footstep on ink score of tones over sonority of storm,
across the boundary.
Down to new century,
blink out core of cones beyond a conformity of norm.

Ink-brushing strokes of starlight,
foot onto one single sight,
root upon the bingo right,
night after night,
time in life runs tight,
long way trumpet a morning bright.

No touchy notes can express:
Keyboard inside nourish heart,
keys touching nudely hard,
with no rest, to theme my best!

[December 2005]

Note: Sonatina is a smaller-sized and simpler sonata. At the time in drafting this one of my earliest pieces, I never came up a "sonority scale" or "sonnet" form in my mind. Bearing the aesthetics of orchestral sonority, I explored sonic chemistry to voice a note on my unsung passion.

ON WINGS OF GRAND DRAGON

Outsider beings
siding a belt potted,
foot via another entry.
Flourishing over quick paces,
a bound clicked to Chinoiserie mood.
Chinatown, a ground cracked to foot,
multi races of nourishing faces.
Root on mom's country.
inside a melting pot
being by being.

Long run
materialized well,
to map sewed mystery,
home for de civiliance.
Heartbeat from the billions cultivated to hear,
landmarks of de cool, adventure, thru pipa tablature.
Marking of kung fu, acupuncture, with art miniature,
cultural beat spans over few thousand of year,
town of the brilliance,
a map of new century,
crystallized bell
of big fun.

Many accents:
Hello, my and all dear,
dragon dances core to core,
potting to call beyond de count, voiced so differently.
Pot to recall for thy hometown, families and families,
lanterns trance at the lore,
greetings of the Year,
a tiny action.

Bigger winner,
longing to nail-form
a specific brand station,
apprehended to go across,
motion away from alcoholic,
crystallizing town's civiliance!
Thou individualized brilliance,
a passion being workaholic,
capable hands crossing
grand Pacific Ocean,
long journey from
Greater China.

Side for no secession,
reasons all will recount,
gonging by de very bright.
With all ages, an aged town,
a bound clicked to Chinoiserie mood,
town of the brilliance, on wings of a Grand Dragon.
Home for civiliance, piloting rings of brand wagon,
Chinatown--a ground cracked to foot.
Beyond the stage joy found,
off the gong for any fight,
passion never go down,
siding for concession.

Chinatown, a ground cracked to foot,
multi races of nourishing faces.
Root on mom's country.
inside a melting pot,
being by being.
Outsider beings
siding a belt potted,
foot via another entry.
Flourishing over quick paces,
a bound clicked to Chinoiserie mood.

Marking of kung fu, acupuncture, with art miniature,
cultural beat spans over few thousands of year,
town of the brilliance,
map of new century,
crystallized bell
of big fun.
Long run
materialized well,
to map sewed mystery,
home for de civiliance.
Heartbeat from the billions cultivated to hear,
landmarks of de cool, adventure, thru pipa tablature.

Pot to recall for thy hometown, families to families,
lanterns trance at the lore,
greetings of the Year,
a tiny action.
Many accents:
Hello, my and all dear,
dragon dances core to core,
potting to call beyond de count, voiced so differently.

Thou individualized brilliance,
passion being workaholic,
capable hands crossing
grand Pacific Ocean,
long journey from
Greater China.
Bigger winner,
longing to nail-form
a specific brand station,
apprehended to go across,
motion away from alcoholic,
crystallizing town's civiliance!

Home for civiliance, piloting rings of brand wagon,
Chinatown--a ground cracked to foot.
Beyond the stage joy found,
off the gong for any fight,
passion never go down,
siding for concession.
Side for no secession,
reasons all will recount,
gonging by de very bright.
With all ages, an aged town,
a bound clicked to Chinoiserie mood,
town of the brilliance, on wings of a Grand Dragon.

[First version in 2005, revised in 2010]

Notes: Chinatown, for many generations, has long been a ground for both the outsiders and insiders to foot on for a commonly recognized direction: Preserving the root. I reviewed a six-strophic ("Six" in Chinese means unlimited in numbering) Chinese poems composed by Mr. Wang Xi Dao 王世道, namely *"Brilliance the Dragon and Home of the Dragon"* 龍的風彩龍的家 under New York Chinatown Series of the *Chien Kuan Magazine*. Due to the gap of phonetic nuisances, especially the rhymes structured within a Chinese poetic form, and the difference of linguistic expression, I turned to sponge my inspirations gained from Mr. Wang's fluent pen-strokes; I attempt to picture our mutual heartfelt admiration onto a vast spectrum of foot journey, one after the another, toned by a score of easily ignored notes.

A RECITATIVE ON STRINGING

Above our heads,
            moon is the same.
   Ocean bisects,
we're playing different game.

Perhaps a voiceful passion can't be sung,
'cause the fateful motion has been hung!

Plucking a bel canto brook'g voice by hand after hand,
knuckling no falsetto crook'g joyance to comprehend.

         No mail delivery can express,
Stringing from my heart: All the best!

[November 2004]

Note: Recitative is a speech-like vocal style generally employed to narrate a prose text. In pairing with brook and crook, falsetto, contrasting to bel canto, means false singing in Italian; it is an artificial method of voice projection for reaching high notes above the singer's natural range. In Chinese culture, moon symbolizes a spirit of purity and a connective link of communication among poets and wanderers.

About the Author

Chan Wing-chi 陳詠智, a Washingtonian poet cum musician, is also an arts practitioner for global communities.

During his tenure as Development Director for the Washington, DC Youth Symphony Orchestra, he raised multi–millions to operate the Orchestra's international tours to Europe and Asia. His artistic/cultural advisory spectrum has been crossing over the ocean, including serving as a consultant for the National Endowment for the Arts, New Jersey and South Carolina Arts Commissions, D.C. Mayor's Office, Jiangsu Provincial Performing Arts Group and China National Symphony; D.C. Commissioner for National & Communities Services; Project Director for Meet The Composer New Residencies Program; Vice President for Washington Symphony Orchestra's Board; commentator for Canada's Fairchild Radio and Voice of America; organizer for Asia Pacific Life Insurance Underwriters Association Conference and Aetna Sales Congress; adjunct professor of music at Green Mountain College in Vermont and Shenyang Conservatory of Music in China, as well as external examiner for Master's thesis at New York University.

As a professionally qualified interpreter for litigation of civil/criminal/domestic/immigration/ patent/finance/traffic cases for the U.S. Department of Justice and federal/state courts, Chan has been admitted to serve as an expert witness for language and cultural analysis by the D.C. Superior, Michigan and Virginia Circuit Courts.

Chan presented academic papers on music and culture at various higher education institutions: Columbia University, Kingston University in London, Tenri University in Japan, University of Hong Kong, Pennsylvania State University, University of District of Columbia, US Library of Congress, to name a few. Chan's Chinese poems and articles have been published under the Asian Research Center of the University of Hong Kong, *Hong Kong Literature, Hong Kong Economic Journal, Mingpao Monthly, Master-Insight.com, Beijing CCT Press,* and various Chinese media.

In 2007, Chan, as choral conductor, took a team of twelve American vocalists to participate in a *Memorial Concert for the 70th Anniversary of Nanking Massacre,* which included Thomas Young, who has been praised as one of the best three American tenors today.

2007, At Nanjing Memorial Concert as Choral Conductor

At the Library of Congress with Grace Cavalieri

With 92-year-old composer Chou Wen-chung

With DCYouth Orchestra Program alumni

www.ingramcontent.com/pod-product-compliance
Lightning Source LLC
Chambersburg PA
CBHW062133160426
43191CB00013B/2287
* 9 7 8 0 9 8 6 4 3 5 3 9 3 *